The Equilibrium Investor

A Capital Operating Manual for Building a Balanced Global Stock Portfolio

Build from strength. Operate with discipline. Compound through equilibrium.

Allan Poulin

The Equilibrium Series™

Copyright Page

The Equilibrium InvestorTM

A Capital Operating Manual for Building a Balanced Global Stock Portfolio

First Edition | July 2026

ISBN: [Your ISBN Number Here]

Publisher: [Your Publishing Imprint Name]

Printed in the United States of America

For permissions inquiries: [your contact email]

Professional Disclaimer

This book is for educational and informational purposes only. Nothing herein should be construed as individualized financial, investment, legal, tax, accounting, retirement, or professional advice.

All investing involves risk, including possible loss of principal. Dividends can be reduced or eliminated. Diversification and asset allocation do not guarantee profit or prevent loss.

The examples, frameworks, portfolio categories, allocation discussions, and company references are provided to explain concepts, not to recommend any specific investment strategy, security, product, or transaction for any particular reader.

Readers should consider their own financial situation, income needs, tax status, time horizon, risk tolerance, family obligations, business interests, liquidity needs, and investment objectives before making decisions.

Before implementing any strategy discussed in this book, readers should consult qualified professionals, including financial advisors, fiduciary planners, CPAs, attorneys, tax professionals, retirement-plan administrators, and other appropriate professionals.

The Internal Capital Loop, Mega Backdoor Roth, foreign tax treatment, tax-loss harvesting, leverage, and other advanced strategies require plan-specific, tax-specific, and legal review. Not all plans permit every technique. Laws, rules, and plan documents change.

The author and publisher assume no responsibility for investment decisions made by readers. This book is a capital operating framework, not a substitute for professional advice.

Dedication

For Jessica.

For building, carrying, cooking, healing, mothering, believing, and making our life richer than any portfolio ever could.

And for our children.

May you learn that money is a tool, discipline is freedom, patience is strength, and the richest life is the one ordered toward what matters most.

Acknowledgments

This book was shaped by more than markets. It was shaped by family, business, aviation, medicine, entrepreneurship, faith, travel, mistakes, discipline, and the daily work of trying to build a life with purpose.

First, I am grateful to my wife, Jessica. She is not only my wife and the mother of our children, but also my partner in building, risking, serving, and continuing forward when the path is not easy. Her discipline, intelligence, resilience, and care have influenced far more of this book than she may realize.

I am grateful for our children, who remind me daily that money is not the point. It is a tool for formation, freedom, education, experience, service, and family strength. Children have a way of revealing whether our systems are truly ordered. They make theory practical very quickly.

I am grateful for the lessons learned through aviation, where discipline, preparation, checklists, and calm decision-making are not abstract virtues. They are operating requirements.

I am grateful for the lessons learned through accounting, business operations, entrepreneurship, and medical practice management, where ideas must eventually become processes, contracts, cash flow, execution, and accountability.

Finally, I am grateful for the reader willing to think differently. This book is not about chasing excitement. It is about building a system, using money as a tool, and becoming the kind of person who can own wealth without being owned by it.

Author's Foreword

This book is not a promise of market outperformance. It is a discipline.

The Equilibrium Investor was written for the person who wants to stop reacting to markets and start building a system. It is for the investor who understands that wealth is not created by excitement alone, that quality still matters, that patience still matters, and that money should serve a life larger than an account balance.

This is not a book about chasing the next hot stock. It is not a book about predicting recessions, timing bottoms, or finding secret investments no one else understands. It is a book about building from strength.

The ideas in these pages are drawn from business, accounting, operations, aviation, entrepreneurship, family life, and the daily discipline required to make decisions under uncertainty. The central premise is simple: a portfolio should be engineered, operated, monitored, and corrected like a serious system.

If this book succeeds, the reader will not merely ask, "What should I buy?" He will ask better questions: What am I building? What role does this asset serve? Does this improve equilibrium? Am I acting from strength or pressure? What does this dollar need to do inside the system?

Reader Note

You do not need to build the entire Equilibrium system at once. Start where you are.

A new investor may begin with broad ETFs, regular contributions, cash reserves, and a simple allocation map. A more experienced investor may use individual companies, dividend strategies, tax-aware account placement, fractional shares, and gain harvesting. A business owner, physician, entrepreneur, or high-income household may need a more customized version of the system.

The principles scale. Do not let complexity prevent action. Begin with purpose. Build the map. Fund the system. Use quality components. Respect cash. Size positions with humility. Reinvest dividends with intention. Diagnose before acting. Write rules before the storm.

Contents

Introduction - Please Walk

In medicine, when the alarm sounds, the amateur wants to sprint. The heart rate rises, the hallway narrows, and every instinct says move faster. But the best operators in high-stakes environments know a different truth: speed without control is not discipline. It is noise.

My wife, Jessica, has a phrase that belongs in every operating room, every cockpit, every boardroom, and every brokerage account: very seldom in life and in medicine is there a true emergency; please walk.

Please walk does not mean ignore the problem. It means arrive with your brain still working. It means breathe, look, listen, diagnose, and act. It means do not let panic spend the attention required to solve the problem.

Aviation teaches the same lesson in different words. Maintain aircraft control. Analyze the situation. Take appropriate action. Land as soon as conditions permit. The order matters. If you stop flying the airplane because you are fascinated by the warning light, the warning light wins.

My father put it in a way I have never forgotten: Don't panic until it's time to panic. The older I get, the more I understand the deeper truth. There is never time to panic. There is only time to maintain control, diagnose, communicate, and act.

That is the heart of this book. The Equilibrium Investor does not chase movement. He builds a system. He does not treat symptoms with random trades. He diagnoses causes. He does not collect impressive stocks. He engineers a portfolio. He does not use money as a trophy. He uses it as a tool to build a stronger life.

Most investors begin with the wrong question: What should I buy? That question feels practical, but it is premature. It skips diagnosis, purpose, structure, cash, risk, account location, position size, tax friction, and behavior. It jumps straight to the transaction before defining the system.

The better question is: What am I building? A portfolio is not a junk drawer of attractive companies. It is a capital operating system. Every holding should have a role. Every dollar should have a job. Every reserve should have a purpose. Every action should improve equilibrium.

This book grew from a life of operating systems. Accounting teaches that numbers must reconcile. Business management teaches that strategy must become process. Aviation teaches that stress punishes improvisation. Medical practice teaches that symptoms are not causes. Family life teaches that money is not the point, but a tool for building a life that matters.

The promise of this book is not that every investment will work or that every market will be beaten. That would be a sales pitch, not a system. The promise is better thinking, better architecture, better behavior, and a repeatable way to assign capital without becoming the greatest risk to your own money.

Build from strength. Operate with discipline. Compound through equilibrium. And when the market gets loud, please walk.

Part I - The Paradigm Shift

Before an investor chooses companies, he must change the question.

Chapter 1 - The Chaser and the Engineer

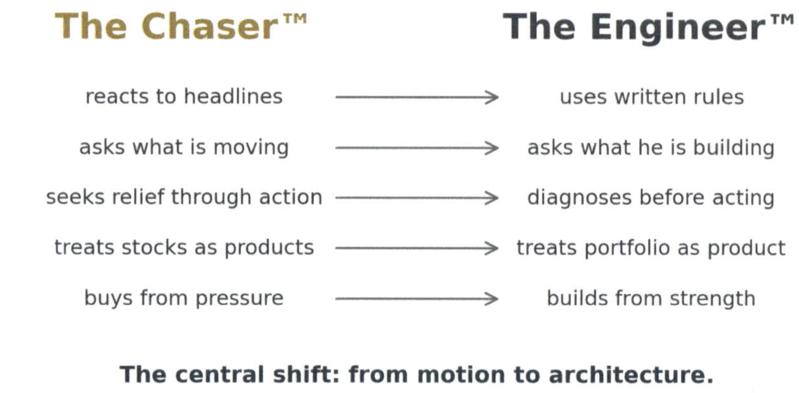

Figure 1. The Chaser-to-Engineer shift: from reactive motion to designed architecture.

The financial world breeds the Chaser. The Chaser is not always reckless. He may be intelligent, hard-working, educated, and successful. But his investing behavior is reactive. He chases performance, headlines, themes, fear, excitement, income, safety, growth, and whatever worked most recently.

The chase may be wrapped in research, charts, podcasts, newsletters, or confident language. The behavior is still the same: motion before architecture.

The Engineer begins differently. He does not ask what is moving. He asks what he is building. That single question changes the entire game. It moves the investor from prediction to design, from emotion to structure, from scattered holdings to a portfolio that operates like a serious system.

A pile of materials is not a house. A shelf full of impressive reef equipment is not a reef. A list of excellent companies is not automatically a portfolio. The parts matter, but the arrangement matters too. A great pump, a great light, and a great salt mix can still fail if the chemistry, flow, livestock, maintenance, and patience are out of balance.

Investing works the same way. A great company can be the wrong purchase if the position is too large, the valuation is stretched, the account location is inefficient, the dividend is not safe, or the investor does not understand what role the holding is supposed to serve.

The financial services industry benefits when investors confuse activity with sophistication. Activity can create fees, spreads, taxes, subscriptions, and dependence. The Engineer understands that the goal is not to look busy. The goal is to build something durable.

Engineering begins with purpose, constraints, and failure points. What is the portfolio for? What risk can the household actually carry? What reserves are required? What role does each sleeve serve? How large can any position become? What happens when prices fall? What happens when life changes? The answers must exist before pressure arrives.

This is not a rejection of opportunity. It is a rejection of disorder. Markets will always offer movement. Most movement does not deserve capital. Some movement does. The difference is diagnosis.

The Chaser looks at blue-chip companies, dividend growers, global leaders, REITs, Treasuries, and hard assets and says, boring. The Engineer looks at them and says, structural integrity.

Equilibrium is not passivity. It is disciplined readiness. It allows the investor to move from strength instead of pressure, trim success without abandoning ownership, buy weakness without catching falling knives, use cash without worshiping cash, and enjoy life without turning money into a trophy.

Footstomp
Stop chasing movement. Start engineering equilibrium.

Chapter 2 - The Portfolio Is the Product.

The stock is not the product. The portfolio is the product.

This sounds simple, but it changes everything. A great company can still be the wrong purchase if the size is wrong, the account is wrong, the valuation is wrong, the role is redundant, or the investor is buying from emotion. The question is not whether a company is impressive in isolation. The question is whether it improves the system.

Most investors admire individual companies. The Equilibrium Investor evaluates relationships between holdings. One company may provide dividend growth. Another may provide defensive stability. Another may provide international exposure. Another may provide real estate income. Cash may provide optionality. Gold may provide a hard-asset hedge. No part should be judged entirely alone.

Diversification is not owning many names. Diversification is owning different sources of return, risk, income, geography, currency, liquidity, and behavior. Ten companies that all depend on the same economic force may be less diversified than five assets with distinct roles.

A portfolio is more like a product than a shopping basket. It should be designed, tested, monitored, improved, and maintained. The investor should know what the product is supposed to do. Income? Growth? Stability? Opportunity? Family wealth? Business resilience? Retirement? Stewardship? The answer shapes the design.

This also means loyalty belongs to the system. A stock may be loved by the market, praised by analysts, and owned by respected investors. It still must earn its seat. If it does not serve the system, admiration is irrelevant.

The Equilibrium Investor does not ask, "Do I like this company?" He asks, "What job would this company perform inside my portfolio, and is it the best tool for that job?"

That one question can prevent years of clutter.

Equilibrium Note
A portfolio is not a junk drawer of attractive companies. It is a designed product. Assign capital, or capital will drift.

Chapter Principles

The stock is not the product; the portfolio is the product.

A good company can be a poor fit.

Diversification is not repetition disguised as variety.

Loyalty belongs to the system.

The stock is not the product. The portfolio is the product.

Chapter 3 - Build From Strength.

The worst financial decisions are usually made from pressure. Pressure to recover. Pressure to keep up. Pressure to look successful. Pressure to act because everyone else is acting. Pressure to solve a problem that should have been prepared for before the problem arrived.

The Equilibrium Investor builds from strength because strength creates options. Cash creates options. Low debt creates options. Quality holdings create options. A written plan creates options. A spouse or advisor who understands the rules creates options. A watchlist creates options. Routine creates options.

Aviation teaches this clearly. In an emergency, the first priority is to maintain aircraft control. Then analyze the situation. Then take appropriate action. Then land as soon as conditions permit. Panic does not help. Panic consumes the resources needed to solve the problem.

My dad used to say, "Don't panic until it's time to panic." It was memorable because it sounded like permission to wait until the proper moment. But the older I get, the more I think the deeper lesson is this: there is never time to panic. By the time panic feels justified, the situation already demands thought, control, judgment, and action. Panic adds nothing. It spends the very attention needed to solve the problem.

The same is true in investing. When markets fall, the first job is not to trade. The first job is control. Maintain discipline. Analyze the situation. Take appropriate action. Restore equilibrium as conditions permit.

Jessica has a similar practical wisdom in medicine and in life: very seldom is there a true emergency; please walk. That does not mean symptoms are ignored. It means the first response is not chaos. A falling price, dividend cut, headline, or recession forecast may require review. It does not automatically require panic.

Build from strength means creating the conditions for good decisions before the hard moment arrives. Pay yourself first. Spend less than you earn. Keep cash reserves. Avoid bad debt. Invest consistently. Use tax-advantaged accounts wisely. Control fees. Own quality. Diversify intelligently. Reinvest income. Do not chase. Do not panic.

Low-hanging fruit is still fruit. The basics are not beneath the serious investor. They are the foundation that lets advanced decisions work.

The answer is often in the room. But the investor must be calm enough to see it.

Equilibrium Note
Don't panic until it's time to panic - and in investing, there is never time to panic.

Panic consumes the attention needed to solve the problem. Build the system before stress arrives.

Chapter Principles

Build reserves before emergencies.

Rules written in calm govern stress.

Cash and routine create options.

The basics are not beneath serious investors.

Build from strength. Do not wait for panic to design the system.

Chapter 4 - Money Is a Tool, Not a Trophy.

Money is a tool, not a trophy.

This principle protects the investor from one of the most expensive forms of disorder: performing success instead of building strength.

A trophy is displayed. A tool is used. A trophy seeks admiration. A tool creates capability. A trophy can become fragile because it depends on what others think. A tool becomes powerful because it helps the owner do something worthwhile.

This is where many people quietly lose the plot. They begin with the honest desire to build wealth, but somewhere along the way wealth becomes a costume. The car becomes the proof. The watch becomes the proof. The house, the vacation, the dinner, the visible lifestyle - all of it becomes evidence offered to strangers that the person has arrived.

But evidence is not equity.

A gold watch can be beautiful. A fine car can be enjoyable. A great hotel, excellent wine, tailored clothing, and a memorable dinner can all have a rightful place in a well-ordered life. The Equilibrium Investor does not reject beauty, comfort, travel, excellent meals, or well-made things. He rejects disorder. Luxury is not evil. Luxury purchased at the expense of freedom becomes a master.

A person can look wealthy and still be fragile. He can drive the right car, wear the right watch, and live in the right neighborhood while having no cash reserve, too much debt, poor retirement funding, no written plan, and no margin for a bad month. That is not wealth. That is a stage set.

Real wealth is often invisible. It may look like an older car that is paid for. It may look like automated contributions. It may look like a boring emergency fund. It may look like private education, a funded retirement account, a business reserve, low-interest debt handled responsibly, or the ability to tell a bad opportunity no.

Money can buy stability, time, education, freedom, business opportunity, experiences, generosity, resilience, and the ability to wait. It can also buy status, appetite, debt, comparison, and anxiety. The difference is order.

The Equilibrium Investor wants excellent things when excellent things serve the life. He does not want expensive symbols that force the life to serve them.

This is why spending must be judged like investing. What is the return? Not merely the financial return, but the human return. Does this purchase create freedom, memory,

beauty, family strength, education, capability, health, generosity, or peace? Or does it merely perform success?

Money should serve the life. The life should not serve the money. This is why the portfolio must be connected to purpose. Otherwise, the investor may compound dollars while losing peace, family, health, or meaning.

The goal is not to have the largest pile. The goal is to use capital well. To provide. To build. To teach. To serve. To create freedom. To live with prudence and gratitude.

The Equilibrium Investor does not worship money. He does not despise it. He uses it.

Equilibrium Note
A tool is judged by what it helps build. Money should build capability, not merely display success.

Chapter Principles

Money is a tool, not a trophy.

Wealth should create capability.

Luxury is not evil; disorder is.

Real wealth is often invisible.

A gold watch can be beautiful; it should not become the master.

Money is not the master. Money is not the trophy. Money is the tool.

Part II - The Distinguished Pool

The Equilibrium Investor begins with quality, proven components, and assets that have earned attention before asking whether they deserve capital.

Chapter 5 - Vetted Components: Why Quality Comes First.

The market contains thousands of securities. The Equilibrium Investor does not begin with all of them. He begins by narrowing the field.

A serious builder does not invent every component from scratch. A reef keeper does not design his own pump, salt mix, heater, and light unless he has a reason. He chooses proven equipment and arranges it into a stable ecosystem. The investor can do the same.

Dividend Kings, Dividend Aristocrats, Dow-style blue chips, global leaders, developed-market champions, REITs, Treasury reserves, gold ETFs, and broad index funds can serve as hunting grounds. They are not purchase orders. A hunting ground says, "Start here." It does not say, "Buy everything here."

Quality is a filter, not a guarantee. A company can have a long dividend record and still become overvalued, overleveraged, or strategically weak. A famous company can disappoint. A global leader can become a value trap. The investor still must examine valuation, balance sheet strength, payout ratio, free cash flow, account location, tax treatment, sector exposure, and role.

But beginning with quality reduces the odds of wasting time on fragile stories. Speculation begins with possibility. Quality begins with evidence.

The Equilibrium Investor wants durable value, not novelty. Novelty may have a place, but it should not be the foundation. The foundation should be built from companies and assets that have survived scrutiny, competition, recession, and time.

Do not reinvent the wheel when the wheel has survived the road.

> **Equilibrium Note**
> *Use proven components, but do not buy blindly. Quality earns attention, not automatic capital.*

Chapter Principles

Start with quality hunting grounds.

A vetted list is not a purchase order.

Quality reduces noise but does not remove analysis.

Novelty should not be the foundation.

Use vetted components. Build from quality. Do not make the foundation speculative.

Chapter 6 - Boring Is Often Where Discipline Lives.

Investors are drawn to excitement. Exciting companies make better stories. They promise disruption, transformation, and the possibility of extraordinary returns. Excitement is not automatically bad, but it is often overpaid for.

Boring is often where discipline lives.

A company that sells essential products, raises prices modestly, manages debt carefully, pays dividends, and compounds quietly may never dominate headlines. It may still create excellent long-term value. A business does not need to be exciting to be excellent.

The Equilibrium Investor respects innovation, but he invests in execution. A story is not a business. A business has customers, margins, cash flow, capital allocation, management, and resilience. Stories can move prices. Businesses fund dividends and compounding.

Patience is more than a virtue. It is a competitive advantage. Many investors cannot tolerate boredom long enough to let compounding work. They jump from one theme to another, always searching for the next dramatic thing. In doing so, they often sell what is working quietly to buy what is exciting loudly.

The same lesson applies to life. Bad relationships, bad partnerships, bad contracts, bad debt, and bad investments are often easier to enter than to exit. Slow is not the enemy. Slow can be thought replacing impulse.

Compounding is quiet. Foundations are quiet. Good routines are quiet. Most durable wealth is built in places that do not entertain the impatient.

Do not confuse excitement with excellence.

> **Equilibrium Note**
> *Boring may be where discipline, cash flow, and compounding live. Patience is a competitive advantage.*

Chapter Principles

Attention is not return.

Stories are not businesses.

Dividend discipline matters.

Slow can be thought replacing impulse.

Do not confuse excitement with excellence. Boring is often where discipline lives.

Chapter 7 - The Global Investor's Advantage.

A domestic-only portfolio can feel safe because it feels familiar. Familiarity is not the same as diversification.

The United States is a remarkable market, but the world is larger than one country, one currency, one index, and one national story. Capital crosses borders. Companies sell globally. Consumers live globally. Innovation, infrastructure, medicine, banking, energy, luxury goods, manufacturing, and food all exist beyond domestic boundaries.

Living outside one's own country teaches what a domestic-only portfolio can hide. The world is not an abstraction. It is made of businesses, workers, currencies, customers, ports, banks, hospitals, families, and governments. Global exposure can add currency diversification, sector balance, dividend variation, valuation opportunity, and participation in economic strength outside the home market.

But global investing must be disciplined. Currency risk matters. Withholding taxes matter. Accounting standards matter. Political risk matters. Liquidity matters. Simplicity matters. A U.S.-listed international ETF may be the right tool. An ADR may be appropriate. Direct foreign ownership may be useful only when the added complexity earns its place.

The Equilibrium Investor is globally aware, not globally chaotic. He uses international exposure to strengthen the system, not to decorate it.

Home bias may be practical, but it should be examined. The question is not whether the investor should own everything everywhere. The question is whether the portfolio depends too heavily on one market when quality exists beyond it.

The world is larger than one market. Use that truth carefully.

Equilibrium Note
Global exposure should strengthen equilibrium, not complicate it. Complexity must earn its seat.

Chapter Principles

The world is larger than one market.

Global exposure can diversify currency, sector, valuation, and policy risk.

Use simple vehicles when simple works.

Global awareness is not global chaos.

Use global exposure to strengthen the system, not complicate it.

Chapter 8 - Every Company Must Earn Its Seat.

A watchlist is not a portfolio.

This is one of the most important distinctions in the Equilibrium method. The watchlist is where interest lives. The portfolio is where capital lives. Interesting companies should not consume real capital until they earn it.

A company does not deserve a seat because it is famous, large, in an index, owned by others, or admired by the investor. It deserves a seat only if it serves a role, fits the map, is sized properly, and offers acceptable value relative to risk.

Admiration is not analysis. A good company can be too expensive. A strong brand can be redundant. A dividend payer can be unsafe. A global leader can create tax complexity. A business can be excellent and still not belong in the portfolio.

Every holding carries costs: capital, attention, risk, tax consequences, opportunity cost, and emotional weight. A crowded portfolio is not automatically diversified. It may simply be clutter.

Before buying, the investor should know the role. Income? Dividend growth? Defensive stability? International exposure? Currency diversification? Inflation resistance? Real estate income? Growth? Cash optionality? If the role cannot be stated, the seat has not been earned.

This is also why starter positions matter. Not every commitment should begin at full size. A company can begin on the watchlist, earn a starter position, prove its role, and eventually earn standard or core status. Commitment should match conviction.

The portfolio is a boardroom. Every seat matters. Every company should be there because it contributes.

> **Equilibrium Note**
> *Do not let interesting companies consume real capital. The portfolio is not a popularity contest.*

Chapter Principles

A watchlist is not a portfolio.

Every holding has cost.

Role comes before purchase.

Commitment should match conviction.

Every holding must earn its seat.

Part III - Engineering the Portfolio

Part III turns quality into structure: balance, a map, position sizing, cash, and account architecture.

Chapter 9 - Balance Before Buying.

Most investors buy first and organize later. They accumulate positions, then attempt to explain the portfolio after the fact. That is not construction. It is cleanup.

The Equilibrium Investor balances before buying. He defines what the system should look like before capital is committed. Balance includes purpose, asset type, sector, geography, currency, income, growth, liquidity, tax location, position size, and routine.

Bull markets disguise poor design. When everything rises, almost any collection of assets can feel intelligent. Stress reveals structure. A portfolio that looked diversified may reveal hidden concentration. Cash may be too low. Growth may dominate. Income may depend on one sector. International exposure may be decorative rather than useful.

Balance is not decoration. It is risk assignment.

A practical Equilibrium Map might include U.S. dividend quality, U.S. blue-chip core, international developed blue chips, global defensive leaders, REITs, gold or hard assets, quality growth, and cash/Treasury reserve. Each sleeve has a target, a band, and a purpose.

The exact percentages can vary by age, income, tax situation, business ownership, family obligations, and temperament. The principle does not vary: define the system before buying the pieces.

Children get out of balance when routine disappears. Businesses drift when process disappears. Portfolios drift when architecture disappears.

Do not buy random stocks. Build your own disciplined index.

> **Equilibrium Note**
> *Balance is architecture. It should exist before the purchase, not after the problem.*

Chapter Principles

Balance before buying.

Hidden concentration is the enemy.

Purpose sets architecture.

Routine protects the system.

Do not buy random stocks. Build your own disciplined index.

Chapter 10 - The Equilibrium Map.

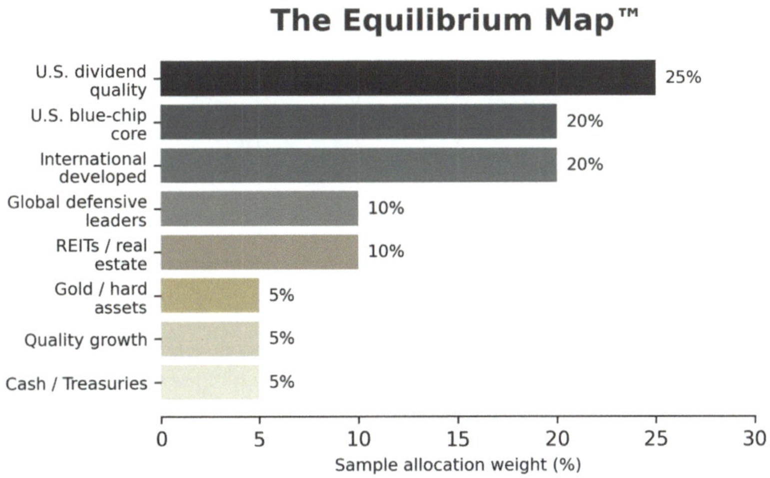

Figure 2. Sample Equilibrium Map allocation. Illustrative only; not individualized advice.

A portfolio needs a map.

The map turns philosophy into allocation. It tells capital where it belongs and gives the investor a standard against which drift can be measured. Without a map, every market move becomes a debate. With a map, movement becomes information.

The Equilibrium Map is not a public index copied blindly. It is a private index: a custom, rules-based portfolio organized around the investor's purpose. It may begin with ETFs and a few core holdings. Over time, it can grow into 25, 50, 75, or 100 holdings, each serving a role.

A sample mature map might be 25% U.S. dividend quality, 20% U.S. blue-chip core, 20% international developed blue chips, 10% global defensive leaders, 10% REITs or real estate, 5% gold or hard assets, 5% quality growth or innovation, and 5% cash/Treasury reserve.

This is not a prescription. It is a starting architecture. The investor may adjust based on age, income, tax situation, business needs, and risk tolerance. The important point is that every sleeve has a job.

The map also reduces decision fatigue. When new contributions arrive, the investor asks which sleeve needs capital. When dividends arrive, he asks where the fuel belongs. When a winner grows, he asks whether the sleeve is overweight. When weakness appears, he asks whether the sleeve is underweight and the thesis remains intact.

A map protects the investor from the moment. It turns emotion into assignment.

Equilibrium Note
The map turns every dollar into an assignment. It protects the investor from improvising under pressure.

Chapter Principles

A private index is a rules-based custom portfolio.

Every sleeve needs a purpose.

The map reduces decision fatigue.

The map makes drift visible.

Do not collect stocks. Build your own disciplined index.

Sleeve	Sample Weight	Role
U.S. dividend quality	25%	Durable income and dividend growth
U.S. blue-chip core	20%	Core American business strength
International developed blue chips	20%	Global and currency diversification
Global defensive leaders	10%	Healthcare, staples, essentials
REITs / real estate	10%	Property, housing, infrastructure, income
Gold / hard assets	5%	Monetary and geopolitical hedge
Quality growth / innovation	5%	Upside without domination
Cash / Treasury reserve	5%	Liquidity and optionality

Chapter 11 - Position Sizing: Conviction Without Concentration.

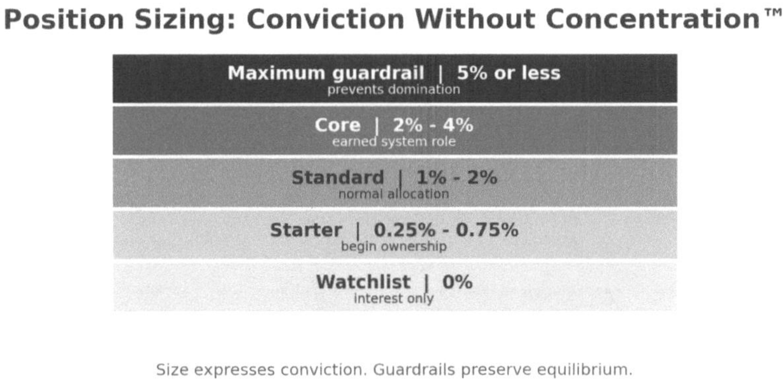

Figure 3. Position sizing is humility made visible.

Conviction is not concentration.

This principle protects the investor from his own best ideas. A company can be excellent, a thesis can be sound, and a position can still become too large. Success creates risk when a winner grows beyond its role.

Position sizing is humility made visible. It admits that even strong analysis can be wrong, early, incomplete, or surprised by events. The goal is not to avoid conviction. The goal is to express conviction without allowing any single company to dominate the system.

The Equilibrium Investor uses categories: watchlist, starter position, standard position, core position, full position, and maximum position. A starter position may be less than 1%. A standard holding may be 1% to 2%. A core holding may be 2% to 4%. Many individual companies may have a maximum around 5% or less, while diversified ETFs may be larger.

The exact numbers can vary. The discipline does not. Every holding needs a target and a maximum. No single company should become the portfolio's personality.

Position size should reflect role, quality, volatility, confidence, balance sheet risk, account location, and correlation with other holdings. A speculative holding, if allowed at all, should remain too small to threaten the system.

Fractional shares make this discipline practical. The investor can trim excess, add gradually, and keep allocations aligned without all-or-nothing decisions.

The Equilibrium Investor wants upside without dependence. He wants ownership without captivity.

> **Equilibrium Note**
> *Position sizing is humility made visible. It protects the investor from needing to be perfectly right.*

Chapter Principles

Conviction is not concentration.

Every holding needs a target and maximum.

No holding should become the portfolio personality.

Fractional shares make sizing practical.

Believe with discipline. Size with humility.

Position Type	Typical Size	Purpose
Watchlist	0%	Interesting, not owned
Starter	0.25% - 0.75%	Begin ownership and study behavior
Standard	1% - 2%	Normal holding with defined role
Core	2% - 4%	High-quality system component
Full	4% - 5%	Upper individual allocation
Maximum	5% or less	Guardrail for most companies
Broad ETF / fund	5% - 20%	Diversified sleeve exposure
Speculative, if allowed	0.25% - 1%	Must never threaten the system

Chapter 12 - Cash Is Loaded Optionality.

Cash is often misunderstood.

In bull markets, cash looks lazy. It sits while stocks rise. It earns less than equities. It can make the investor feel like he is falling behind. But cash held with purpose is not laziness. It is loaded optionality.

Cash allows the investor to act when opportunity appears. It prevents forced selling. It supports household and business obligations. It gives the portfolio a reserve of controlled energy that can be deployed when conditions justify action. Cash is boring until everyone else needs it.

The Equilibrium Investor separates cash by purpose. Household emergency cash is not investment capital. Business operating cash is not speculation capital. Tax reserve cash is not opportunity cash. Portfolio opportunity cash is designed for rebalancing, buying quality weakness, and preserving optionality.

This distinction matters. A family or business that confuses reserves can weaken itself at the exact moment strength is needed.

Cash also supports the internal capital loop. When possible, a family or business can build enough internal reserves to borrow from itself, invest in its own business, children, systems, education, or opportunity, then repay that capital with discipline and, where appropriate, interest. The point is not to reject all borrowing. The point is to keep more control, optionality, and value inside the family system when it is prudent and properly documented.

Cash has risk. Inflation can erode it. Fear can cause an investor to hold too much. But a portfolio with no cash can become brittle. The right level creates strength without starving compounding.

Cash is not the destination. It is the staging ground. It is not the engine. It is reserve fuel.

> **Equilibrium Note**
> *Cash held with purpose is freedom waiting for assignment.*

Chapter Principles

Cash creates options.

Different reserves have different jobs.

Cash prevents forced selling.

Internal capital can strengthen the family or business system when properly governed.

Cash is not laziness when it has a job. Cash is loaded optionality.

Chapter 13 - Account Architecture and the Wealth-Manager Tax

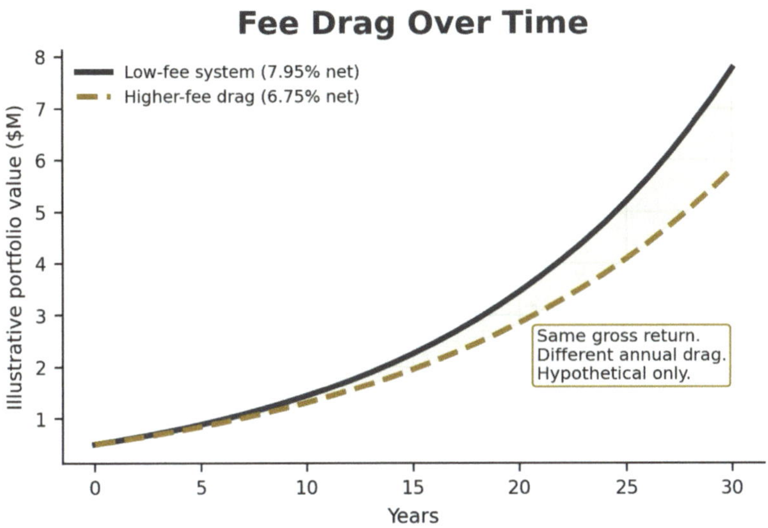

Figure 4. Fee drag illustration. Same gross return, different net compounding. Hypothetical only.

The portfolio is not only a list of holdings. It is also an account architecture. Where an asset lives can matter almost as much as what the asset is. Taxable brokerage accounts, Traditional IRAs, Roth IRAs, workplace plans, HSAs, business retirement plans, and cash vehicles each create different rules for liquidity, taxes, compounding, reporting, and flexibility.

This chapter is not tax advice. It is a framework for asking better questions with qualified professionals. The Equilibrium Investor does not blindly place assets wherever there is room. He asks what each container does best and what kind of activity belongs inside it.

A taxable account can provide flexibility, liquidity, potential capital-gains treatment, foreign tax credit considerations, charitable gifting opportunities, and access before retirement age. It can also create tax friction when the investor trades too much. The taxable account rewards patience, tax awareness, and disciplined harvesting.

A traditional tax-deferred account may provide current tax advantages and long-term compounding, but withdrawals are generally taxed later. It may be useful for assets that generate ordinary income, for broad compounding, and for retirement accumulation, depending on the household's situation. Required rules, future tax rates, and withdrawal planning matter.

A Roth account is different. When used properly, it can become a tax-free runway for long-term compounding. For investors whose workplace plans allow after-tax contributions and in-plan Roth conversion or in-service distribution, the strategy often called the Mega Backdoor Roth may create an additional path into Roth space. The details depend entirely on plan design and current law. The rule is simple: do not assume; verify with the plan document and tax counsel.

The Roth wrapper is especially powerful for assets expected to compound for a long time or for strategies that may involve more frequent calibration, because qualified growth is sheltered from future tax. That does not make reckless trading wise. It simply means the account can reduce tax friction when the system calls for disciplined action.

Fees also deserve diagnosis. A one percent annual advisory fee sounds small until it compounds for decades. A household paying high AUM fees should know exactly what it receives: planning, tax coordination, estate strategy, behavioral coaching, business planning, investment management, or merely a standard ETF allocation dressed in expensive language.

Professional advisors can be valuable. The enemy is not advice. The enemy is unexamined fee drag. A strong CPA, attorney, financial planner, or fiduciary advisor may be worth far more than the cost when the advice prevents mistakes, improves tax structure, coordinates estate plans, or protects the family system. But a fee should earn its seat just like a company earns its seat.

The Equilibrium Investor does not ask, Can I avoid every fee? He asks, Does this fee improve equilibrium? Does it buy expertise, protection, discipline, tax efficiency, legal structure, or time? Or does it simply reduce the compounding engine while outsourcing decisions I could operate with a written system?

Account architecture is where the operating manual becomes practical. Contributions enter through the right doors. Dividends are assigned intentionally. Trims happen where tax friction is acceptable. Cash reserves remain properly separated. Retirement wrappers are used with humility and precision. Fees are reviewed as structural leaks.

Footstomp

Taxes, accounts, and fees are not side issues. They are part of the machine. Give every asset the right container, and make every fee earn its seat.

Fee Drag Illustration - Same gross return, different annual drag. This is hypothetical and not a prediction.

Assumption	Low-Fee System	Higher-Fee System
Starting balance	$500,000	$500,000
Annual contribution	$25,000	$25,000
Assumed gross return	8.00%	8.00%
Annual advisory/platform drag	0.05%	1.25%
Net annual return used	7.95%	6.75%
Illustrative value after 30 years	$7.93M	$6.35M
Illustrative difference	-	$1.58M less before taxes

Part IV - Operating the System

The system must be funded, fueled, calibrated, and maintained through routine.

Chapter 14 - Dollar-Cost Averaging: The Discipline of Showing Up.

Most investors want the perfect entry point. The problem is that the perfect entry rarely feels perfect when it arrives. When prices are high, the investor worries he is overpaying. When prices fall, he worries they will fall further.

Dollar-cost averaging breaks the trap of perfect timing. It means investing a set amount at regular intervals rather than waiting for emotional certainty. It does not guarantee the highest possible return in every circumstance. It provides behavioral structure.

It makes the investor show up.

A portfolio cannot compound capital that never enters the system. A beautiful map and strong watchlist are useless if the engine is not funded. Pay yourself first. Do not wait to see what is left after lifestyle consumes the month.

Inside the Equilibrium system, new contributions are not random. They are calibration tools. If international exposure is underweight, the next contribution can go there. If cash is below target, the next contribution can rebuild optionality. If a quality holding is below its band and the thesis remains intact, new money can add without requiring a sale elsewhere.

Routine matters. Families function better with routine. Businesses function better with process. Aviation uses checklists and flows. A reef system depends on repeated maintenance. Investing is no different.

The Equilibrium Investor is not someone who invests only when excited. He is someone who funds the system in good markets, bad markets, boring markets, and uncertain markets.

The habit is the engine.

> **Equilibrium Note**
> *Dollar-cost averaging is not only a math technique. It is a behavioral discipline.*

Chapter Principles

The system must be funded.

Pay yourself first.

New contributions are calibration tools.

Routine reduces timing pressure.

Show up consistently. The habit is the engine.

Chapter 15 - Dividends: Fuel for the Machine.

A dividend is not just income. It is fuel.

A dividend can be spent, reinvested, accumulated, redirected, used to rebalance, used to rebuild cash, or used to buy temporary weakness in another part of the portfolio. Every dividend is a decision point.

The conventional investor asks, "How much does this yield?" The Equilibrium Investor asks whether the dividend is supported by cash flow, whether the payout ratio is sustainable, whether debt is manageable, whether management is disciplined, and whether the yield is attractive because the business is strong or because the market expects trouble.

Yield alone can be dangerous. A high yield may be opportunity. It may also be a warning. The business funds the dividend. Study the business first.

Dividend growth can be more valuable than yield alone because it may signal increasing cash flow, discipline, and confidence. The goal is not the largest check today. The goal is durable and growing fuel for the machine.

Dividends also help behavior. In flat or volatile markets, income gives the system something to do while price waits. Reinvested dividends buy more shares when prices are lower. Redirected dividends can strengthen underweight sleeves. Pooled dividends can rebuild cash.

As the portfolio matures, dividend assignment becomes strategic. Automatic reinvestment can be useful, especially early. But a mature system should ask where the fuel does the most good.

Dividends are fuel. Do not chase them. Do not waste them. Assign them.

Equilibrium Note
Income gives the system something to do while price waits.

Chapter Principles

A dividend is fuel.

Yield alone is not enough.

The business funds the dividend.

Dividend cuts require diagnosis.

Do not chase yield. Use dividends as fuel for equilibrium.

Chapter 16 - Fractional Shares: The Modern Calibration Tool.

Fractional shares changed how precisely a disciplined investor can operate.

In the past, small investors often had to buy whole shares. High-priced stocks could distort allocation. Small dividends might sit idle. Rebalancing could be clumsy. Today, fractional shares allow the investor to place exact dollar amounts where the system needs them.

That precision matters because the Equilibrium Investor is not trying to make dramatic all-or-nothing decisions. He wants to calibrate. Trim a little. Add gradually. Start a position carefully. Reinvest a dividend exactly where it belongs. Reduce exposure without abandoning ownership.

Fractional shares allow the investor to separate ownership from exposure. He can still own a great company while reducing the amount of portfolio risk tied to it. He can preserve the engine and harvest the excess.

But the tool can be misused. Fractional shares can encourage fidgeting: tiny trades made to relieve anxiety rather than improve the system. The map must govern the tool. The investor should ask whether an action restores balance or merely creates the feeling of action.

Calibration restores balance. Fidgeting relieves anxiety.

Used within the system, fractional shares allow the investor to build a private index, add in stages, reinvest small dividends, and operate with precision that earlier generations lacked.

Precision reduces drama.

> **Equilibrium Note**
> *Fractional shares are modern. The discipline must be timeless.*

Chapter Principles

Fractional shares make precise calibration possible.

Do not abandon ownership when exposure can be calibrated.

Calibration is not fidgeting.

The map governs the tool.

Use fractional shares to calibrate, not to fidget.

Chapter 17 - Gain Harvesting Without Abandonment.

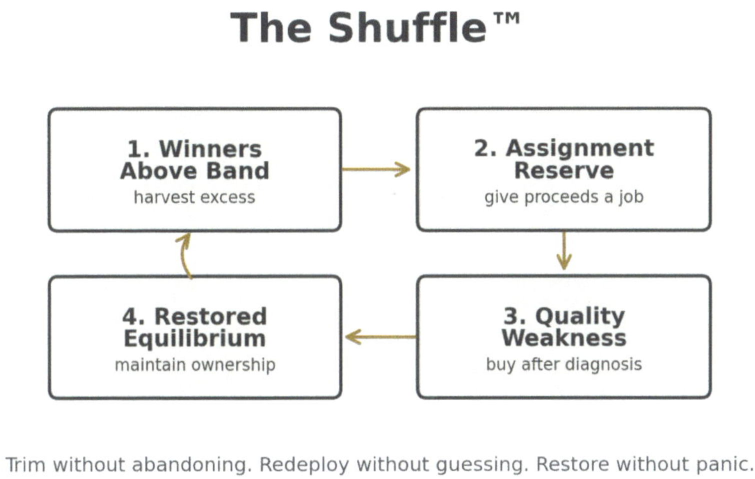

Figure 5. The Shuffle: harvest excess, assign proceeds, buy diagnosed weakness, restore equilibrium.

A rising stock creates a good problem: success. The company performs well, the price rises, and the position grows. The investor feels validated. But success can create imbalance.

Gain harvesting is not abandoning a winner. It is trimming excess appreciation when a position moves beyond its intended role, then redeploying that excess into the rest of the system.

Harvest the excess. Preserve the engine.

Many investors think they must either hold forever or sell completely. The Equilibrium Investor uses a third option: trim. Trimming allows ownership to continue while reducing excess exposure. It protects the system from unconscious dependence.

A winner that grows from 2% to 3% may simply be succeeding. A winner that grows from 2% to 10% may become the portfolio's personality. That is different.

Gain harvesting should be governed by target bands, tax awareness, valuation, and diagnosis. A trigger is not an automatic sell. It is a command to review. Has the business improved enough to justify a larger role? Has the price risen faster than value? Would the capital improve equilibrium elsewhere?

A trim is not complete when the sale executes. It is complete when the proceeds are assigned. They may rebuild cash, fund an underweight sleeve, buy quality weakness, or wait in Treasuries.

The investor's loyalty belongs to equilibrium, not to any single winner.

> **Equilibrium Note**
> *Do not punish winners. Prevent success from becoming imbalance.*

Chapter Principles

Gain harvesting is not abandonment.

A winner can become too large.

Tax friction matters.

Proceeds must be reassigned.

Harvest the excess. Preserve the engine.

Chapter 18 - Buying Weakness Without Catching Falling Knives.

A lower price is not automatically a bargain.

Sometimes weakness is opportunity. Sometimes weakness is warning. The difference is diagnosis.

The Equilibrium Investor does not buy weakness merely because something is down. He buys weakness only when the original thesis remains intact, the position still belongs in the system, and the lower price improves expected return without introducing unacceptable risk.

Temporary weakness may come from market corrections, sector rotations, temporary earnings disappointment, interest-rate pressure, currency movement, or investor overreaction. Permanent impairment may come from broken competitive advantage, debt stress, lost relevance, dividend collapse, management failure, fraud, or a business model that no longer works.

Buy temporary weakness. Avoid permanent impairment.

The investor should ask: would I buy this today if I did not already own it? That question strips away attachment. Adding to a position should not be an argument with the market or an attempt to defend ego. It should be a capital allocation decision.

Staged buying is useful because the investor does not know the bottom. He may add one-third when the thesis is intact and the position is below target, another third if price falls further but diagnosis remains favorable, and the final third after confirmation.

The watchlist is the shopping list for disciplined weakness. Preparation should happen before panic arrives.

Buy weakness from strength. Never from desperation.

> **Equilibrium Note**
> *A falling price is a symptom, not a diagnosis.*

Chapter Principles

Cheap is not the same as undervalued.

Buy temporary weakness, not permanent impairment.

Use staged buying.

The watchlist prepares the investor before panic.

Do not buy the dip blindly. Buy weakness only after diagnosis.

Chapter 19 - The Constant Calibration Cycle.

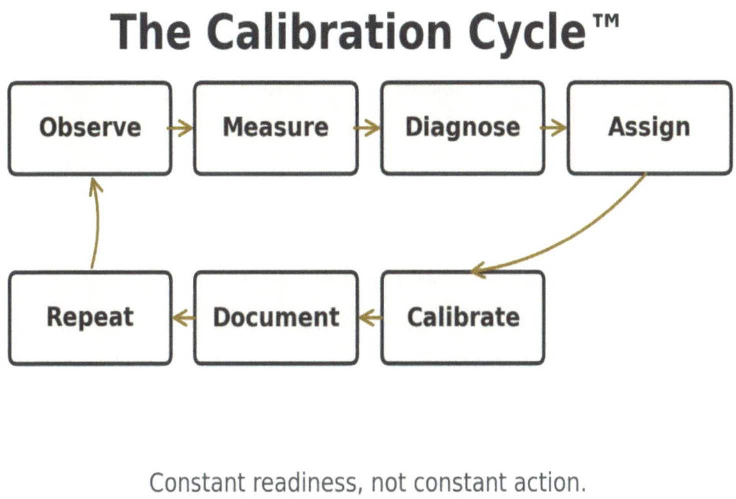

Figure 6. The Calibration Cycle: observe, measure, diagnose, assign, calibrate, document, repeat.

A portfolio should breathe. It should not thrash.

The Constant Calibration Cycle is how the Equilibrium Investor keeps the system aligned without reacting to every movement. The cycle is simple: observe, measure, diagnose, assign, calibrate, document, repeat.

Observation is not obsession. Measurement turns feeling into information. Diagnosis separates action from reaction. Assignment gives every dollar a job. Calibration makes the adjustment. Documentation keeps the investor honest. Repetition turns discipline into routine.

This cycle coordinates the operating tools. Dollar-cost averaging supplies capital. Dividends supply fuel. Fractional shares provide precision. Gain harvesting captures excess. Buying weakness redeploys into quality after diagnosis. Cash provides optionality.

Without a cycle, the tools become disconnected. Contributions may be random. Dividends may be ignored. Fractional shares may encourage fidgeting. Gain harvesting may become nervous selling. Buying weakness may become catching knives. Cash may become fear.

The system determines urgency. The market does not.

Routine protects family life too. The portfolio should not consume the investor's attention to the point that it steals from the life it was built to serve. A review rhythm allows engagement without obsession.

The Equilibrium Investor cannot control the market. He can control his behavior. That is enough.

Equilibrium Note
Calibration is not constant action. It is constant readiness.

Chapter Principles

A portfolio should breathe, not thrash.

Measurement turns feeling into information.

Every dollar needs assignment.

Doing nothing can be calibration.

Observe. Diagnose. Calibrate. Let the portfolio breathe, but do not let it thrash.

Part V - Discipline, Risk, and Diagnosis

The investor learns to separate symptoms from causes, use checklists, vet commitments, stress-test leverage, sell broken theses, and avoid overactivity.

Chapter 20 - Symptoms Are Not Causes.

A symptom tells you where to look. It does not tell you what to do.

A stock price falls. A yield spikes. A sector lags. A dividend is cut. A position becomes overweight. A headline creates fear. Each is a symptom. None is a complete diagnosis.

The conventional investor treats symptoms as instructions. A stock falls, so he sells. A stock rises, so he buys. A yield rises, so he chases. The Equilibrium Investor pauses. He asks what changed, why it changed, whether the thesis remains intact, and whether action would improve equilibrium.

Never prescribe a trade before making a diagnosis.

In medicine, treating the wrong symptom can delay the right intervention. In aviation, reacting before understanding can create a worse emergency. Investing is similar. Urgency is dangerous when it replaces thought.

A falling price may be opportunity or danger. A rising price may be strength or overvaluation. A high yield may be income or warning. The same symptom can justify buying, holding, trimming, selling, or waiting depending on cause.

Internal emotions are symptoms too. Fear, greed, envy, regret, boredom, overconfidence, and the urge to check the portfolio constantly all deserve attention. They do not deserve automatic obedience.

The system should be stronger than the mood.

> **Equilibrium Note**
> *A symptom tells you where to look. It does not tell you what to do.*

Chapter Principles

Symptoms are not causes.

Never prescribe a trade before diagnosis.

Internal emotions are symptoms too.

The system should be stronger than the mood.

Do not treat the symptom. Diagnose the cause.

Chapter 21 - The Root-Cause Checklist.

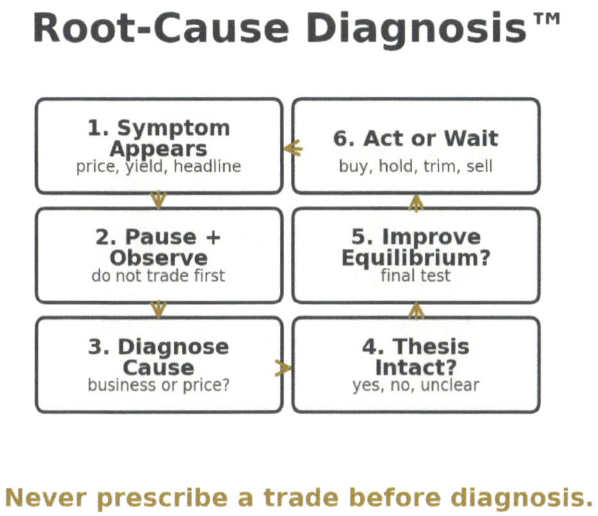

Figure 7. Root-cause diagnosis keeps the system stronger than the mood.

A checklist is not a substitute for intelligence. It is a protection for it.

Serious environments use checklists because pressure makes intelligent people skip steps. The Root-Cause Checklist exists to create a disciplined pause between symptom and action.

The investor should ask: What exactly happened? Why did it happen? Did the business change or only the price? Is the thesis intact? What role does the holding serve? Is the position within its target band? Would I buy this today? Am I acting from strength or pressure? What are the tax, fee, and account consequences? What happens if I am wrong? Does this action improve equilibrium?

These questions are not meant to make investing complicated. They are meant to prevent expensive simplicity.

The same discipline applies beyond the portfolio. A person should not enter a marriage, business partnership, contract, debt structure, or investment because the beginning feels exciting. Commitments are easier to enter than unwind. Wise people ask hard questions before commitment.

Patience before commitment is usually cheaper than regret after commitment.

The checklist should be concise enough to use and serious enough to matter. Brevity should concentrate value, not remove depth.

The investor writes the questions before the emergency appears.

Equilibrium Note
The checklist protects intelligence under pressure.

Chapter Principles

Do not act until you know why you are acting.

Would I buy this today?

Patience before commitment matters.

The final test is equilibrium.

Use the checklist. Find the cause before committing capital.

Chapter 22 - Relational Equilibrium: Commitments, Contracts, and Patience

Patience is not only an investing virtue. It is a life virtue. It protects capital, relationships, contracts, partnerships, businesses, and families. Many people lose more money through bad commitments than they ever lose in the stock market.

The Equilibrium Investor understands that every major commitment has a balance-sheet effect. Marriage, partnership, debt, employment contracts, business agreements, leases, guarantees, acquisitions, practice arrangements, and investor relationships can all either strengthen the system or quietly load it with hidden liabilities.

It is almost always easier to enter a relationship than to unwind it. The beginning is emotional, exciting, and full of possibility. The exit is legal, expensive, slow, public, and often damaging. That is true in marriage. It is true in business. It is true in contracts. It is true in investing.

In Catholic marriage preparation, couples are often asked to slow down and answer serious questions before they make a permanent commitment. They discuss values, children, money, family, expectations, sacrifice, faith, conflict, and the life they intend to build. A mediator helps reveal whether the couple actually knows what they are agreeing to.

The principle is universal even for readers who do not share the faith tradition: ask hard questions before commitment. Use a mediator, advisor, attorney, CPA, mentor, spouse, or experienced operator to expose what emotion may hide. Do the diagnostic before signing the contract.

Consider the high-earning professional who makes an extraordinary income but carries the financial consequences of repeated relational mistakes. On paper, the income looks powerful. In reality, alimony, child support, legal expenses, lifestyle inflation, and emotional exhaustion can leave very little freedom at the end of the month. The income became a treadmill for old decisions.

Consider the person who works brutal overseas rotations to earn capital while a misaligned partner spends everything before he returns home. The problem is not income. The problem is system misalignment. Capital enters the household and immediately leaks through values that were never reconciled.

Children are a blessing. Life is a learning lab. No human system is perfect. But responsibility requires honesty. If a commitment can create long-term obligations, it deserves pre-flight inspection. If the values are incompatible, the cheapest and wisest decision may be to walk away before signatures, vows, guarantees, or debt make the problem expensive.

The same rule applies to stocks. Start small when possible. Get to know the company. Watch management. Understand the role. Let the position earn its way from watchlist to starter to standard to core. Do not give full capital to an untested relationship because the beginning feels exciting.

Relational equilibrium means commitments are sized, vetted, and aligned. The investor who learns this principle in the portfolio may begin to see it everywhere. Good relationships compound. Bad relationships compound too. Choose carefully.

Footstomp

The cheapest mistake is the one you never make. Ask hard questions before commitment. Patience before entry is cheaper than regret after exit.

Chapter 23 - Leverage Without Captivity

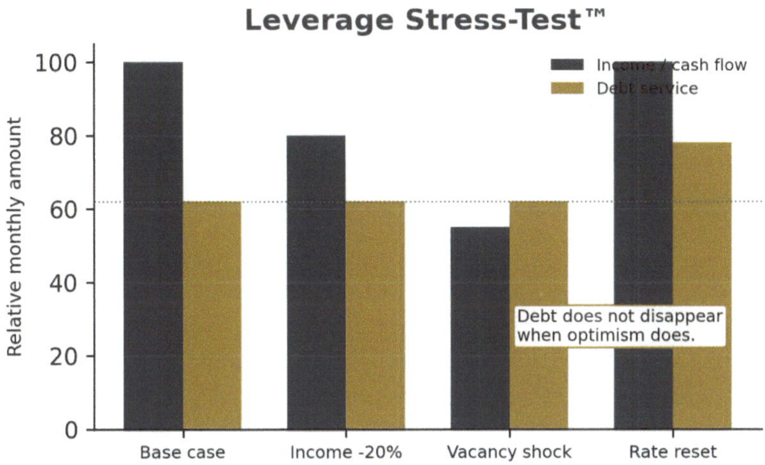

Figure 8. Leverage must be stress-tested before it is used.

Leverage is a powerful tool, not a personality trait. Used wisely, it can accelerate ownership, business growth, real estate acquisition, and investment returns. Used emotionally, it can turn a manageable mistake into a system-threatening failure.

The Chaser sees leverage as proof of ambition. The Engineer sees leverage as load. He asks how much stress the structure can carry when conditions stop cooperating.

The classic example is the investor who owns twenty rental properties with heavy debt. In good conditions, the story sounds brilliant. Tenants pay the notes, inflation reduces the real burden of debt, equity builds, and the owner appears to be scaling rapidly. But what happens if a major employer leaves town? What happens if several tenants stop paying? What happens if rates reset, insurance rises, repairs cluster, or the local market goes cold?

The rent may disappear. The note does not. Interest does not care about optimism. Taxes, insurance, repairs, and vacancies do not wait for confidence to return. The leverage that looked intelligent on the way up can become an anchor on the way down.

This is not an argument against all debt. It is an argument against fragile debt. A mortgage can be reasonable. A business line can be useful. A margin facility can be tempting but dangerous. A leveraged ETF can be a specialized tool but should never be confused with a durable foundation. The question is always the same: can the system survive the downside without forced selling, family stress, or loss of control?

The Equilibrium Investor uses a leverage stress test before borrowing. What happens if income falls by twenty percent? What happens if rates rise? What happens if tenants leave? What happens if the asset drops thirty percent? What happens if the business has a slow quarter? What happens if I cannot refinance? What happens if the lender changes the terms?

Leverage must be matched to reserves. It must have a repayment plan. It must be documented. It must be sized so that the investor can sleep, think, and act from strength. If the only way the leverage works is under perfect conditions, the system is not engineered. It is hoped.

The same principle applies inside a stock portfolio. Margin can magnify gains, but it can also force liquidation at the worst possible time. Leveraged funds can magnify a tactical view, but daily reset, volatility drag, and compounding behavior can surprise investors who do not understand the instrument. Complexity must earn its seat, and leverage must earn it twice.

The purpose of wealth is freedom. Leverage that creates captivity has failed, even if it made the investor look aggressive for a season.

Footstomp

Use leverage only when the downside is covered. Debt should serve the system, not hold the family hostage.

Chapter 24 - When to Sell Completely.

The Equilibrium Investor prefers ownership, but ownership is not blind loyalty.

Sometimes the right answer is to sell completely. Selling is appropriate when the reason for ownership no longer exists, when risk has changed permanently, when the holding no longer serves its role, or when capital can serve the system better elsewhere.

Panic selling is emotional escape. Disciplined selling is system maintenance.

The first reason to sell is a broken thesis. If the dividend grower cannot support the dividend, the defensive company has lost stability, the REIT's balance sheet has become fragile, or the global leader has lost competitive advantage, the original reason for ownership may no longer hold.

The second reason is permanent impairment. A lower price does not repair a broken business. A familiar brand does not repair lost relevance. A long history does not guarantee recovery.

The third reason is loss of role. A company may remain good but no longer serve the system. Not every sale is an accusation. Sometimes capital can work better elsewhere.

The purchase price should not control the current decision. The market does not care what the investor paid. The better question is: would I buy this today if I did not already own it?

A sale is complete only when the capital is reassigned. Selling is not merely removal. It is reallocation.

> **Equilibrium Note**
> *Never let nostalgia become an allocation strategy.*

Chapter Principles

Preference for ownership is not blind loyalty.

The investor's loyalty belongs to the system.

Temporary weakness can be held; permanent impairment needs honesty.

A sale requires reassignment.

Hold quality patiently. Trim success carefully. Sell broken theses decisively.

Chapter 25 - The Cost of Overactivity.

Doing more is not the same as doing better.

Activity feels productive. Buying feels decisive. Selling feels protective. Research feels responsible. Watching the market feels engaged. But a portfolio can be damaged by too much attention.

Every action has a cost: taxes, fees, spreads, short-term gains, wash-sale complications, poor execution, decision fatigue, emotional exhaustion, strategy drift, complexity, and time taken from family, business, health, and life.

Overactivity is a leak.

The Equilibrium Investor is active where activity serves the map. He contributes, reinvests, trims excess, buys weakness after diagnosis, sells broken theses, reviews the dashboard, and documents major decisions. But he does not touch the portfolio merely to feel involved.

Calibration restores balance. Fidgeting relieves anxiety.

Financial media, apps, and social platforms are designed to provoke motion. The trade button is always available. Availability is not instruction.

The portfolio is not built for entertainment. It is built for purpose.

Some of the best decisions are decisions not to act. Stillness can be discipline when the system is healthy.

> **Equilibrium Note**
> *Calibration restores balance. Fidgeting relieves anxiety.*

Chapter Principles

Doing more is not doing better.

Every action has a cost.

Overactivity destroys feedback.

Sometimes nothing is the correct action.

Do not confuse activity with discipline. Move only when movement improves equilibrium.

Part VI - The Equilibrium Investor Constitution

The calm self writes the rules. The stressed self follows them.

Chapter 26 - Writing the Rules Before the Storm.

The worst time to design rules is during the storm.

When markets are calm, the investor can think clearly. He can define purpose, choose allocations, set cash targets, write position-size limits, and decide when to buy, trim, sell, or wait. When markets are falling, fear enters the room and begins negotiating.

Pressure is a poor author.

The Equilibrium Investor Constitution is the written operating document for the portfolio. It defines purpose, authority, boundaries, process, and acceptable behavior. It answers the questions emotion will ask later.

What am I building? What belongs? What does not belong? How much cash should I hold? How large can a position become? When do I add? When do I trim? When do I sell? How do I use dividends? How do I handle leverage? What do I do when markets decline?

The calm self should write the rules. The stressed self should follow them.

The constitution begins with purpose, then defines the map, position sizing, cash policy, contributions, dividend policy, gain harvesting, buying weakness, selling, leverage, review rhythm, documentation, counsel involvement, and storm rules.

A constitution should be short enough to use and serious enough to govern. It may evolve when life changes, but it should not be rewritten every time fear shouts loudly.

The investor does not need certainty. He needs a system he can trust when certainty disappears.

> **Equilibrium Note**
> *The calm self writes the rules. The stressed self follows them.*

Chapter Principles

Write rules before the storm.

Purpose governs design.

A portfolio held only in the head is rewritten by mood.

Rules may evolve, but not from panic.

Write the rules before the storm. Do not let panic author the portfolio. There is never time to panic.

Chapter 27 - The Equilibrium Dashboard.

A system needs instruments.

A pilot does not fly by feeling alone. A physician does not practice by instinct alone. A business owner does not manage operations from vibes alone. The Equilibrium Investor should not operate a portfolio by mood.

The dashboard shows whether the system remains aligned with design. It should track sleeve allocation, target-band status, largest positions, sector exposure, geographic and currency exposure, dividend income, cash and liquidity, watchlist opportunities, risk events, capital awaiting assignment, tax exposure, leverage, and behavior.

A good dashboard creates clarity. A bad dashboard creates noise.

If a metric does not help maintain equilibrium, diagnose risk, assign capital, or preserve discipline, it may not belong. More columns do not automatically create more wisdom.

The dashboard should be reviewed on a rhythm. Monthly observation, quarterly calibration, and annual strategic review may be enough. A warning light triggers review; it does not fly the airplane.

The dashboard also protects against false confidence. A rising portfolio does not automatically mean a healthy portfolio. It may hide concentration, low cash, weak dividend quality, or too much growth exposure.

Do not operate by mood. Operate by instruments.

> **Equilibrium Note**
> *The dashboard should show what governs action. Measure what matters. Ignore what merely provokes.*

Chapter Principles

A system needs instruments.

More data does not equal better judgment.

Target bands trigger review.

Behavior is part of performance.

Do not operate by mood. Operate by instruments.

Part VII - The Distinguished Life

The portfolio is not the destination. It is the servant of a larger life.

Chapter 28 - From Portfolio to Lifestyle.

A portfolio is not the destination. It is a tool.

Money is a tool, not a trophy. The investor who forgets this may build wealth and still lose equilibrium. He may become richer and more anxious, more informed and less present, more successful and less free.

The portfolio should support a distinguished life: family strength, education, business opportunity, freedom, generosity, service, health, meaningful experiences, and stewardship.

This is where the book must leave the spreadsheet and enter the house. A family does not experience wealth only as a balance on a statement. It experiences wealth as calm, margin, better choices, fewer forced decisions, a richer table, better education, more time together, and the ability to build from strength.

One of the great blessings in my own life is that my wife is a fabulous cook. Even better, she genuinely enjoys it. That has changed how we think about going out to dinner. We enjoy a night out together, but we have also had the experience of paying the bill, walking to the car, and saying, "It was nice to be out with you, but the food was not as good as what you make at home."

That realization matters. If something can be done better at home, with more care, comfort, better ingredients, and less expense, then going out should have a higher standard. The night out should offer something we cannot easily replicate: an exceptional meal, special ambiance, a memorable experience, a beautiful setting, great service, or some other value that makes the splurge worthwhile.

This is not cheapness. It is discernment.

There is a difference between refusing to spend and refusing to waste. The Equilibrium Investor is not trying to drain joy out of life. He is trying to reserve premium dollars for premium value. If the home table is better, warmer, richer, and more meaningful, then the restaurant must earn the night out.

Investing is no different. Not every available investment deserves capital simply because it is available. Not every cheaper alternative is a good substitute for quality. Sometimes it is better to wait, save, and buy the asset that truly belongs in the system rather than spend capital on something merely acceptable.

A mediocre dinner out is not a bargain just because it is cheaper than a great one. A mediocre investment is not a bargain just because it is easier to afford.

The same is true of status spending. A gold watch, a luxury car, or a beautiful trip may be worthwhile if it fits the life and does not weaken the system. But if the purchase exists mainly to prove something to other people, it should be questioned. The Equilibrium Investor does not ask, "Can I afford this?" only. He asks, "Does this improve the life we are building?"

This question is powerful because many expensive things are affordable and still not worth it. Many modest things are inexpensive and extremely valuable. A dinner at home with an excellent cook, a bottle of wine chosen with care, and children laughing around the table may produce a better return than an overpriced restaurant. A paid-for car may create more freedom than a luxury lease. A funded education account may compound more meaning than another status purchase.

Lifestyle equilibrium means spending, saving, investing, and building with intention. The portfolio map and the lifestyle map should agree. If the portfolio is built for resilience but the lifestyle is built on fragility, the system is out of balance.

This is also where internal capital matters. When possible, a household or business can build enough reserve strength to borrow from itself, invest in itself, its children, its business, its systems, and its future, then repay that capital with discipline. Properly documented and handled with professional advice, the interest and optionality can remain inside the family system rather than automatically being sent to a bank.

This is not an argument against all borrowing. Outside capital can be useful. But the strongest household is not automatically the one with the largest visible lifestyle. It is often the one with the most internal options.

The portfolio should serve the life. The life should be worthy of the portfolio.

> **Equilibrium Note**
> *The investor should not ask only how much the portfolio earned. He should ask what kind of life the capital is helping build.*

Chapter Principles

Money is a tool, not a trophy.

Wealth should increase freedom, not appetite.

A mediocre purchase is not a bargain.

Premium dollars should purchase premium value.

The portfolio should serve the life.

Do not let the tool become the master.

Chapter 29 - The Internal Capital Loop and The Distinguished Life

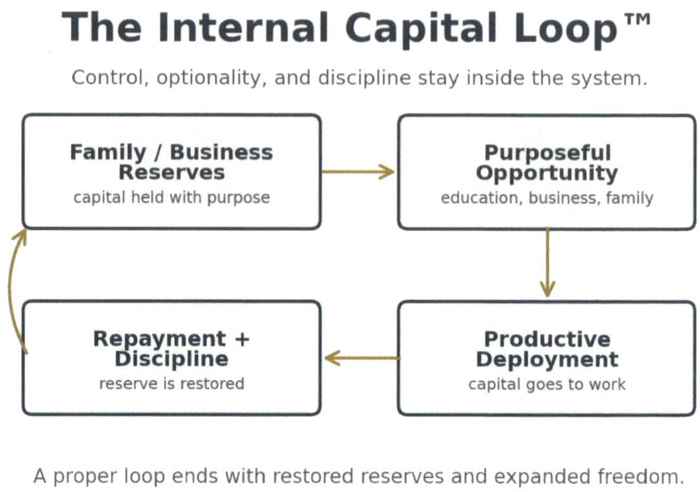

Figure 9. The Internal Capital Loop keeps control and discipline inside the family or business system.

The Internal Capital Loop is the household or business version of building from strength. Instead of automatically running to outside capital for every need, the family system builds reserves, lends to productive purposes when appropriate, documents the transaction, and repays itself with discipline.

This is not a loophole, a gimmick, or a rejection of banks. It is an operating philosophy. Capital that remains inside the family system can preserve control, reduce friction, improve speed, support business opportunities, fund education, and teach responsibility. But it must be governed. Undocumented borrowing from yourself can become nothing more than disguised spending.

A proper internal loop begins with separation. Emergency cash is not opportunity cash. Tax reserve cash is not business expansion cash. Portfolio cash is not vacation cash. Internal capital exists only after the core reserves are protected.

The loop then requires a purpose. What is the capital being used for? Education? A business system? Equipment? A down payment? A temporary liquidity bridge? A family investment? The use should improve the life or the system. It should not become a way to avoid discipline.

The third requirement is documentation. Write the amount, purpose, repayment schedule, interest if appropriate, source of funds, and approval. Involve professionals when legal, tax, retirement, business, or family complexity requires it. Treat internal capital with more respect than bank capital, not less.

Finally, the loop requires repayment. The system should be restored. Capital should flow back so it can be redeployed again. A family that borrows internally and never repays has not created a bank. It has created a leak.

This is how the portfolio becomes a lifestyle without becoming a master. Money funds the system. The system funds the life. The life produces work, learning, service, business, children, meals, memories, and meaning. Capital returns to the system with gratitude and discipline.

That is the distinguished life. Not luxury for its own sake. Not deprivation for its own sake. Not status. Not fear. Distinction is order. Distinction is stewardship. Distinction is knowing why money exists and refusing to let it rule the house.

Luxury can be purchased. Distinction must be formed. A beautiful dinner, a memorable trip, a good bottle of wine, a well-made watch, or a wonderful home can all belong in a well-ordered life. But they must serve the life, not consume it.

The question at the end is not only whether the portfolio grew. The question is whether the investor grew with it. Did the capital serve the family? Did the system create freedom? Did the discipline produce peace? Did wealth become stewardship? Did the portfolio support a life of meaning?

Footstomp

The portfolio is not the destination. It is the servant of a larger life. Luxury can be purchased; distinction must be formed.

Final Manuscript Closing

The Equilibrium Investor does not chase movement. He builds a system.

He does not collect stocks. He engineers a portfolio.

He does not worship yield, growth, cash, gold, real estate, or any single company. He assigns each tool a role.

He does not panic when symptoms appear. He diagnoses causes.

He does not let winners become idols. He harvests excess and preserves the engine.

He does not buy weakness blindly. He buys only after the thesis is confirmed.

He does not confuse activity with discipline. He moves only when movement improves equilibrium.

He writes rules before storms. He operates by instruments. He uses money as a tool, not a trophy.

And he remembers that the portfolio is not the destination. It is the servant of a larger life.

Build from strength. Operate with discipline. Compound through equilibrium. That is the way of The Equilibrium Investor.

The Equilibrium Series begins here because capital is the easiest place to see the operating system. But the same principles belong in the household, the business, the partnership, the contract, the school choice, the mission, the meal, and the life. The goal is not only better investing. The goal is better stewardship.

Appendices

Tools for turning the philosophy into operating behavior.

Appendix A - The Equilibrium Investor Constitution Template

The constitution is the written operating document for the portfolio. It should be short enough to use, serious enough to govern, and clear enough to return to during stress.

Core Sections Purpose statement.

Portfolio map and target ranges.

Position-size rules.

Cash policy.

Contribution policy.

Dividend policy.

Gain-harvesting policy.

Buying-weakness policy.

Selling policy.

Leverage policy.

Internal capital loop.

Review rhythm.

Documentation rules.

Storm rules.

Dad's rule: Don't panic until it's time to panic.

Equilibrium translation: There is never time to panic; there is only time to maintain control, diagnose, and act.

Signature Rule I wrote these rules in calm conditions so they can govern me during stress.

Name: ____

Date: ____

Reviewed annually on: ____

Appendix B - The Equilibrium Map Worksheet

The Equilibrium Map is the target structure of the portfolio. It tells every dollar where it belongs.

U.S. dividend quality _____% _____% - _____% Durable income and dividend growth

U.S. blue-chip core _____% _____% - _____% Core American business strength

International developed blue chips _____% _____% - _____% Global and currency diversification

Global defensive leaders _____% _____% - _____% Healthcare, staples, essentials

REITs / real estate _____% _____% - _____% Property, housing, infrastructure, income

Gold / hard assets _____% _____% - _____% Monetary and geopolitical hedge

Quality growth / innovation _____% _____% - _____% Upside without domination

Cash / Treasury reserve _____% _____% - _____% Liquidity and optionality

Rule: Do not collect stocks. Build your own disciplined index.

Appendix C - Position Sizing Guide

Position sizing is the discipline of deciding how much capital each holding deserves.

Watchlist 0% Interesting, not owned

Starter 0.25% - 0.75% Begin ownership and study behavior

Standard 1% - 2% Normal holding with defined role

Core 2% - 4% High-quality system component

Full 4% - 5% Upper-level individual allocation

Maximum 5% or less Guardrail for most companies

Broad ETF / fund 5% - 20% Diversified sleeve exposure

Rule: Conviction deserves expression, not domination. Size with humility.

Appendix D - Cash Policy Worksheet

Cash is not one thing. It can be emergency protection, business stability, tax reserve, opportunity capital, or internal family financing.

Household emergency cash $_____ $_____ Family protection

Business operating cash $_____ $_____ Payroll, rent, vendors, delays

Tax reserve cash $_____ $_____ Known tax obligations

Portfolio opportunity cash $_____ $_____ Buying weakness and rebalancing

Treasury / money market reserve $_____ $_____ Safe yield and liquidity

Internal capital reserve $_____ $_____ Self-funded family/business lending

Rule: Cash is assigned strength. Give every reserve a job.

Appendix E - Account Architecture Worksheet

Every asset needs a role and every role needs the right container. Before placing a holding, ask where it creates the least friction and the greatest flexibility.

Questions: Is the income tax-inefficient? Is the holding likely to be traded or trimmed? Is long-term compounding the priority? Is liquidity required? Could foreign withholding taxes apply? Are retirement-plan rules understood? Is professional guidance needed?

Rule: The account is part of the machine. Place assets with purpose.

Container	Potential Role	Diagnosis Required
Taxable brokerage	Liquidity, flexibility, tax-aware long-term holdings	Avoid fidgeting; monitor capital gains and foreign tax issues
Traditional IRA / 401(k)	Tax-deferred compounding and retirement accumulation	Future withdrawals taxable; rules can change
Roth IRA / Roth 401(k)	Long runway for tax-free qualified growth	Eligibility and plan rules matter
HSA, if eligible	Tax-advantaged health reserve and long-term optionality	Must follow HSA rules
Cash / Treasury / money market	Reserves, taxes, opportunity, stability	Inflation and purpose drift

Appendix F - Dividend Fuel Tracker

Dividends are fuel. Track the source, quality, tax treatment, and assignment of that fuel.

Estimated annual dividend income $_____

Estimated monthly average $_____

Dividends received year to date $_____

Dividend income growth _____%

Portfolio yield _____%

Before assigning dividend cash, ask: Which sleeve is underweight? Is cash below target? Is the paying company still attractive? Would automatic reinvestment create concentration? Does this assignment improve equilibrium?

Rule: Do not chase dividends. Do not waste them. Assign them.

Appendix G - Gain Harvesting Checklist

Gain harvesting trims excess appreciation without abandoning ownership.

Before trimming, ask: Is the position above target? Is the thesis intact? Has valuation become stretched? Is concentration excessive? Are tax consequences acceptable? Where will proceeds be assigned?

Decision tree: Position above target? If no, hold. If yes, review thesis. If thesis broken, review for sale. If thesis intact and concentration is excessive, measure taxes, trim excess, and redeploy.

Rule: Harvest the excess. Preserve the engine. Redeploy with purpose.

Appendix H - Buying Weakness Diagnostic Checklist

A lower price is not automatically a bargain.

Before adding to weakness, ask: Why did price fall? Is weakness temporary or permanent? Is the thesis intact? Would I buy this today if I did not already own it? Is the sleeve underweight? Is capital available from strength? Will adding violate position limits?

Use staged buying when uncertainty remains. Add gradually. Document the reason.

Rule: Diagnose first. Add only when weakness improves equilibrium.

Appendix I - Selling Decision Checklist

Selling is not failure. Selling is capital reassignment.

A selling review is required when the thesis appears broken, the dividend fails, debt increases materially, management credibility is damaged, competitive advantage weakens, the role disappears, complexity becomes unacceptable, or the holding violates the constitution.

Before selling, ask: Would I buy this today if I did not already own it? Is the impairment permanent? Are taxes understood? What will replace the role? Am I selling from discipline or emotion?

Rule: Sell when the holding no longer deserves its seat. Then reassign the capital.

Appendix J - Overactivity Checklist

Overactivity damages portfolios through taxes, fees, spreads, complexity, decision fatigue, and strategy drift.

Before acting, ask: What system problem does this solve? Is this calibration or fidgeting? What are the tax and fee costs? Can this be solved with contributions or dividends? Can it wait? Does this follow the constitution?

Rule: Do not pay taxes, fees, spreads, and attention costs just to feel busy. Move only when movement improves equilibrium.

Appendix K - The One-Page Equilibrium Dashboard

The dashboard is the investor's instrument panel.

Track: total portfolio value, sleeve allocation versus target, largest holdings, cash reserve, dividend income, capital awaiting assignment, watchlist opportunities, risk events, tax issues, leverage concerns, actions taken, next review date, and behavior check.

Behavior check: Did I follow the contribution plan? Did I assign dividends intentionally? Did I avoid unnecessary trading? Did I diagnose before acting? Did I protect cash reserves? Did I follow the constitution?

Rule: Do not operate by mood. Operate by instruments.

Appendix L - Lifestyle Equilibrium Worksheet

The portfolio should serve the life.

Before major spending, ask: Does this purchase serve our life or perform our life? Does it increase freedom or reduce it? Does it support family, education, health, service, beauty, or meaningful experience? Does it create recurring obligations? Does it weaken the system?

Worth the Splurge Test: Can we do this better at home? Does it offer something we cannot replicate? Is the quality exceptional? Is the ambiance or memory worth it?

Internal Capital Loop: If you borrow from the family system, document it, repay it, and respect it.

Rule: Spend with purpose. Save with discipline. Invest with equilibrium.

Appendix M - The Equilibrium Investor Lexicon

Core Identity Terms

The Chaser™ - An investor driven by emotion, trend-following, and reactive behavior. Focuses on individual stock charts, treats the market like a casino, and operates from pressure rather than strength.

The Engineer™ - An investor who focuses entirely on system design, asset allocation, and mechanical, non-emotional asset maintenance. Treats their portfolio like an aircraft requiring calibrated pre-flight checks.

Please Walk™ - The core principle: when symptoms appear (market drops, headlines, dividend warnings), arrive with your brain still working. Breathe, look, listen, diagnose, and act. Panic consumes the attention needed to solve the problem.

Built From Strength™ - Making all capital allocation decisions from a position of reserves, low debt, quality holdings, and written rules—never from pressure, urgency, or desperation.

Money Is a Tool, Not a Trophy™ - Wealth should create capability and freedom, not merely display success. Luxury purchased at the expense of structural integrity becomes a master rather than a servant.

Mechanical Operating Terms

The Equilibrium Map™ - The definitive, multi-sleeve structural blueprint that dictates the exact weight and operational role of every asset class within the portfolio. Your private index, customized to your household's purpose.

The Shuffle™ - The routine process of fractionally trimming winning, over-allocated assets to immediately purchase high-quality, under-allocated assets experiencing temporary weakness. Continuous buy-low-sell-high without full liquidation.

Target Bands™ - Acceptable allocation ranges around target weights (typically ±2%). When a sleeve drifts outside its band, it triggers review—not automatic panic, but systematic calibration.

The Calibration Cycle™ - Seven-step operational ritual: Observe → Measure → Diagnose → Assign → Calibrate → Document → Repeat. Turns discipline into routine.

Dividend Fuel™ - Dividend income used strategically to reinvest, rebalance, rebuild cash, or support intentional spending. Income gives the system something to do while price waits.

Loaded Optionality™ - Purposeful cash reserves held for liquidity, buying weakness, or emergency protection. Cash is not "lazy"; it is freedom waiting for assignment.

Gain Harvesting™ - Trimming excess appreciation when a position moves beyond its intended role, then redeploying that excess into the rest of the system. Preserve the engine; harvest the excess.

Buying Weakness™ - Adding to positions only when the original thesis remains intact, the position still belongs in the system, and the lower price improves expected return without introducing unacceptable risk. Temporary weakness only, not permanent impairment.

Off-the-Shelf Machinery™ - Pre-vetted, historically proven corporate entities (Dividend Kings, Dividend Aristocrats, DJIA constituents, DAX/FTSE leaders) that require no basic product invention to build secure wealth. Buy the field, not the needle.

Private Index™ - A custom, rules-based portfolio organized into weighted sleeves, distinct from public benchmarks like the S&P 500 or Russell 2000.

Risk And Protection Terms

Symptom vs. Cause™ - A falling price is a symptom. The business condition is the cause. Never prescribe a trade before making a diagnosis. The same symptom can justify buying, holding, trimming, selling, or waiting depending on cause.

Conviction Without Concentration™ - Strong belief in a thesis must never allow any single position to dominate the system. Humility made visible in position sizing. Every holding needs a target and maximum.

The Wealth-Manager Tax™ - AUM fees (typically 1-1.5% annually) as structural leaks in compounding. Over 30 years, 1.25% drag can cost $1.6+ million in lifetime wealth creation versus self-managed zero-fee alternatives.

Relational Equilibrium™ - Marriages, business partnerships, contracts, and leases as balance-sheet items requiring pre-commitment diagnostics. Start small, vet thoroughly, ask hard questions before signatures become expensive regrets.

The Distinguished Life™ - The end goal: freedom, stewardship, meaning, family strength, education, generosity—not just portfolio balance. Money serves the life; the life should not serve the money.

Internal Capital Audit™ - Periodic check on whether spending patterns align with stated values. Are you refusing to spend, or refusing to waste? Does this purchase improve equilibrium or merely perform success?

Storm Rules™ - Rules written in calm conditions, followed during stress. The calm self writes the rules; the stressed self follows them. Never rewrite the constitution when fear shouts loudly.

ADVANCED MECHANISMS (Series Expansion Potential)

Pre-Flight Checklist™ - Root-cause diagnostic executed before any capital commitment. Identical to aviation safety protocols: What changed? Why? Thesis intact? Role defined? Size appropriate? Tax consequences understood? Worst-case scenario survivable?

Equilibrium Dashboard™ - Single-page instrument panel tracking sleeve allocation, target-band status, largest positions, sector/geographic exposure, dividend income, cash reserves, watchlist opportunities, risk events, and behavior score. Do not operate by mood; operate by instruments.

Leverage Stress-Test™ - Downside scenario planning before borrowing. What happens if income falls 20%? If rates rise? If tenants leave? If the asset drops 30%? If refinancing becomes unavailable? Use leverage only when the downside is covered.

Fidgeting™ - Dangerous habit of constantly checking financial applications and making small, ad-hoc, emotional adjustments to relieve personal anxiety rather than executing a pre-planned routine. Calibration restores balance; fidgeting relieves anxiety.

Signature Maxims

"The stock is not the product. The portfolio is the product."

"Don't panic until it's time to panic—and in investing, there is never time to panic."

"Cash is loaded optionality."

"Conviction is not concentration."

"Buying from strength, not desperation."

"Build from strength. Operate with discipline. Compound through equilibrium."

"Calibration restores balance. Fidgeting relieves anxiety."

"Every company must earn its seat."

"Luxury can be purchased; distinction must be formed."

"The answer is always in the room."

"When the market gets loud, please walk."

Appendix N - Relational and Contract Pre-Flight Checklist

Commitments can compound for or against the system. Before entering a marriage, partnership, contract, loan, guarantee, business deal, or long-term obligation, ask serious questions before the emotional momentum becomes expensive.

Do our values align? Do our incentives align? Are money expectations clear? What happens if things go wrong? What are the exit terms? What obligations continue after exit? Who has authority? Who controls cash? What does counsel say? What would make this a bad deal? Can we start small? Are we moving from strength or pressure?

Rule: Start small when possible. Ask hard questions early. The cheapest mistake is the one never signed.

Appendix O - Leverage Stress-Test Worksheet

Leverage should never be judged only by the optimistic case. Stress-test the downside before borrowing or using leveraged instruments.

Ask: What happens if income falls 20%? What happens if rates rise? What happens if tenants leave? What happens if the asset drops 30%? What happens if the business has a slow quarter? What happens if refinancing is unavailable? What happens if the lender changes terms? What cash reserve protects the system? What is the repayment plan?

Rule: Use leverage only when the downside is covered. Debt should serve the system, not hold the family hostage.

About the Author

Allan Poulin brings together professional aviation, accounting, global operations, medical practice management, entrepreneurship, and international business experience to create a disciplined capital operating framework for self-directed investors. He and his wife, Jessica, a Maternal-Fetal Medicine subspecialist, have built and operated medical practices across multiple markets while raising five children and living a life ordered around family, education, stewardship, and disciplined decision-making.

www.ingramcontent.com/pod-product-compliance
Lightning Source LLC
LaVergne TN
LVHW051135210926
848482LV00006B/326

* 9 7 9 8 9 9 6 9 7 1 3 2 9 *